Ducks

by Sara Wilhelm

HOUGHTON MIFFLIN HARCOURT
School Publishers

PHOTOGRAPHY CREDITS: Cover © Mark Duffy/Alamy; 1 © Nature Picture Library/Alamy; 2 © Digital Vision; 3 © Stockbyte/Alamy; 4 © Kenneth H. Thomas/Photo Researchers, Inc.; 5 © Eric and David Hosking/Corbis; 6 © Nature Picture Library/Alamy; 7 © Sean Bolton/Alamy; 8 © David Muench/Corbis; 9 © Bates Little Hales/ Animals Animals/Earth Scenes; 10 © Mark Duffy/Alamy

Printed in China

ISBN-13: 978-0-547-42733-1
ISBN-10: 0-547-42733-6

5 6 7 8 0940 18 17 16 15 14 13 12
4500345273

It is hot now.
The grass is green.

The duck has a nest.
She has new eggs.

The duck sits
on the eggs.

The eggs start
to open!

The new ducks
grow up.

The new ducks swim
in the water.

It is fall now.
The leaves fall down.

8

It is cold now.
Each duck goes away.

The yellow sun gets hot.
The ducks come back.

Responding

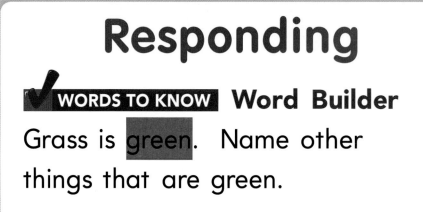

WORDS TO KNOW **Word Builder**

Grass is green. Name other things that are green.

Talk About It

Text to World Where do ducks live? What things are green where ducks live?

WORDS TO KNOW

down	grow
fall	new
goes	open
green	yellow

TARGET STRATEGY Visualize

Picture what is happening as you read.

Level: D
DRA: 6
Science
Strategy:
Visualize
Word Count: 65

1.3.13 Build Vocabulary

HOUGHTON MIFFLIN
Online Leveled Books

ISBN-13: 978-0-547-42733-1
ISBN-10: 0-547-42733-6
90000
9 780547 427331

W8-BIF-852

HOUGHTON MIFFLIN

1431841